AF417088
RYDER'S
CHOCOLATE
Banana
Written By O'Briena Hope

Based on a true story.

In a house not too far,
with walls painted bright,
lived little Ryder,
A boy full of might.
He was clever yet sneaky,
with a twinkle in eye,
and one little secret
that he tried to deny.

One afternoon,
while his mother wasn't around,
Ryder crept quietly
not making a sound.
He tiptoed past toys
and through the hallway,
right to her bedroom
where the chocolate bars lay.

"Just one little bite,"
Ryder thought with a smirk,
"Then I'll put it back,
no one will be hurt."
He grabbed the chocolate,
smooth and sweet,
and took a big bite
of that delicious treat.

When he approached his mother,
she sat with a frown,
looking at evidence
chocolatey brown.
Ryder froze,
with chocolate all on his face,
thinking fast,
he tried to escape the disgrace.

"Did you eat the candy
that I left in my room?"
said Ryder's mother,
and Ryder felt doomed.
"No I didn't, Not today!"
Ryder said.
With chocolate on his face,
his shirt, and his hands.

"Then what's on your face?"
His mother asked.
"I don't know," Ryder said,
quick and fast.
"So, it's not chocolate?"
She asked once again.
"No, it's banana"
Ryder said with a grin.

It was easy to tell
that Ryder told a lie.
"Not today, it's banana"
He continued to deny.
"You did eat the candy,
tell mommy the truth"
"Fine , I did it,"
Ryder said, feeling blue.

"Next time my son,
please ask me first,"
"and don't tell lies,
because lies are the worst"
"OK I'm sorry"
Ryder then apologized.
For stealing the chocolate
and telling the lies.

So remember, young friends,
Always tell the truth.
And don't take things
that don't belong to you.

THE END

Dedicated to Ryder Hope
and all of the children around the world.
With Love, O'Briena "Bri Biase" Hope.

it's
banana